MUSIC

DARREN HENLEY
& TIM LIHOREAU

BOOSEY & HAWKES

London · New York · Berlin · Sydney

Published in 2003 by Boosey & Hawkes
Music Publishers Ltd, in association with
Classic FM

Cover design by Lynette Williamson
Printed and bound in Malta by Interprint Ltd

Introduction

Classic FM has always believed that classical music should be a part of everyone's life. If you already listen to the music we play every day and you want to know more about it, then you've come to the right place.

This is a pocket guide for people with normal-sized pockets. That means it isn't the biggest book about classical music that you'll be able to find. But what it lacks in size, it makes up for in facts, stories and, most important of all, recommendations for great music to listen to.

If you haven't listened to Classic FM yet, then hopefully this book will well and truly whet your appetite, as well as answering some of the questions about classical music that you've always wanted to ask.

Darren Henley
Tim Lihoreau

ADAGIO

This Italian word is a composer's way of telling a performer to play their music very slowly. *Adagio* is slower than *andante* but faster than *largo*. Slow **movements**, in general, are often simply called *"adagios"* because so many bear this marking. Italy was once the centre of the music industry so all the composers wrote the directions in Italian. This continues today, meaning that a German composer writing for a Spanish pianist and a Dutch violinist would still tell them what speed to play in Italian. Odd, but true.

Tomaso ALBINONI (1671–1751)

Best known for his *Adagio for Organ and Strings*, even though it was actually written by an Italian professor in 1958 – the same year as Pele scored a hat-trick in the World Cup in Sweden. It was based on only a fragment of the original manuscript. So, Albinoni wrote hundreds of tunes in his lifetime but is now famous for one he didn't write.

ALLEGRO

A speed instruction from a composer to a performer. The message is to play fast – not, however, as fast as *presto* but faster than *allegretto* (which means allegro-ish). Probably the most famous allegro of all is the "da da da DER . . ." of **Beethoven's** *5th Symphony*.

- **Not to be confused with:** Allegri or the Austin Allegro. The first is a composer born in the 16th century, best known for his choral masterpiece *Miserere*. The second is a 1970s car often favoured by aunties and geography teachers, paradoxically not exactly renowned for being fast

ALTO

Usually, the females who either can't sing as high as **sopranos**, or who can but want a quiet life, free from throat strain. Just as **violas** are the slightly lower, some would say duller, versions of **violins**, so the altos are . . . well, let's leave it there, shall we? Men can be altos too, but . . . well, again, let's just leave it there.

ARIA

This basically means "song". Most of the big hits from **operas** are arias. They are the solos or set pieces performed by singers playing the big roles.

Johann Sebastian BACH (1685–1750)

This German composer was the most famous of a large musical family. Alongside **Handel**, he was one of the greatest composers of the **baroque** period. He was also an organist and church music master, which is why lots of his stuff is religious.

- **Check out:** the *Brandenburg Concertos* | *Toccata and Fugue in D minor* (perfect music for Vincent Price in the film *The Phantom of the Opera*) | *Sheep May Safely Graze*

Samuel BARBER (1910–1981)

One of the most popular American composers, Samuel Barber is best known for his *Adagio for Strings*, which was used to great effect by the director Oliver Stone in his Vietnam War movie, *Platoon*. More recently, his hauntingly beautiful *Violin Concerto*, composed on the death of his mother, has become a firm Classic FM favourite.

- **Not to be confused with:** *The Barber of Seville*, which is an opera by Rossini

BARITONE

The voices of these male singers are higher than **basses**, but lower than **tenors**. So if you can't reach the high notes and have only ever been able to get the low notes first thing in the morning, best become a baritone. The international superstar Bryn Terfel is a fine example of a bass-baritone, whose voices, predictably, lie somewhere between basses and baritones.

BAROQUE

Music written between, roughly, 1600 and 1750 is described as coming from the baroque period. Composers who were producing new material at this time include **Bach**, **Handel** and **Vivaldi**. If you imagine that eras in music are like star signs, with "modern" as Aquarius (genius or mad, hard to tell), "**romantic**" as Cancer (slushy, doe-eyed, dreamy) and "**classical**" as Gemini (sometimes slushy, sometimes not), then "baroque" is clearly the Virgo – neat, tidy, everything in its place, but never too much emotion.

JOHN BARRY (born 1933)

British composer who made his name with his music for **films**. More recently he has had a number of big hits with his CDs of orchestral music. His style is very lush, almost epic, and he has a talent for very hummable tunes.

- **Check out:** *The Beyondness of Things* | *Dances with Wolves*

BASS

The lowest of the male singers, the ones who sound like they've just got up after a heavy night on the sauce. In opera, they don't get as many of the hero roles as the tenors: if this seems unfair, listen to Lee Marvin singing in *Paint your Wagon* and ask yourself – would you elope with him? Incidentally, bass is pronounced "base". Again, quite apt if you remember Lee Marvin's character.

BASSOON

The bassoon is the lowest woodwind instrument of the **orchestra**. It looks something like a didgeridoo wearing too much jewellery, but with an espresso frother coming out of the side. In fact, just like espresso, it too comes in single and double varieties.

Ludwig van BEETHOVEN
(1770–1827)

Along with **Mozart**, Beethoven has a strong claim on the title "the world's greatest classical composer". He wrote everything: **concertos**, **operas**, choral works, pieces for solo instruments – you name it – but his speciality was the **symphony**. He led a tough life, often beaten, early on, by his alcoholic father. In his twenties, his doctor told him that he was going deaf and by the time he was in his thirties, he had totally lost his hearing. The supreme quality of the works which he wrote and never actually heard remains one of the great marvels of classical music.

- **Check out:** *Symphony No. 5,* which must have the most famous opening bars in all classical music | *Symphony No. 6* ('*Pastoral*') | *Symphony No. 9* ('*Choral*') – particularly the magnificent final movement, *The Ode to Joy*

Hector BERLIOZ (1803–1869)

If you are looking for a "patron saint of the **romantic** period", then you could do worse than light upon floppy-fringed Frenchman, Hector Berlioz. Hector was a bit of a luvvie, and, indeed, Hector's house was often home to some rather wild, over-dramatic behaviour. He once pursued an ex-lover with pistols and poison. Another he followed disguised as a maid. Say no more.

- **Check out:** *Symphonie Fantastique* | the oratorio *The Childhood of Christ* | his *Requiem,* which was written for a HUGE chorus and orchestra as well as four brass bands – one at each corner of the stage

Leonard BERNSTEIN (1918-1990)

This American composer's biggest hit was the musical *West Side Story*. Bernstein wrote the music and Stephen Sondheim wrote the words – what a partnership! He also spent a lot of his life touring as a very successful **conductor**.

- **Check out:** his overture to *Candide* and see if you can stop your foot from tapping

Georges BIZET (1838–1875)

Another **romantic** Frenchman. His best-known work is the **opera** *Carmen*. It tells the story of a beautiful woman who not only seduces a soldier only to dump him for a matador, but also works in a cigarette factory. Despite the popularity of *Carmen,* it's another work of Bizet's which is the Classic FM listeners' favourite duet of all time, 'Au fond du temple saint', from his opera *The Pearl Fishers*. Although *Carmen* is a huge hit now, poor Bizet popped his chausseures while it was still a bit of a flop.

Luigi BOCCHERINI (1743–1805)

Boccherini is best known for the *Minuet* from his *String Quintet No. 5,* which is just one of a total of 154 quintets he wrote for various different combinations of instruments. One out of 154. Life can be cruel, can't it?

Alexander BORODIN (1833–1887)

Borodin was only a part-time composer. His day job was as a highly respected scientist in Russia.

As a result, his first published work was a scientific paper, rather than a piece of music. His **opera** *Prince Igor* was actually completed after he had died, by composers **Nikolai Rimsky-Korsakoff** and Alexander Glazunov.

- **Check out:** *Polovtsian Dances* from *Prince Igor* | *In the Steppes of Central Asia* | *On the Action of Ethyl Iodide on Hydrobenzamide and Amarine* (his first work)

Johannes BRAHMS (1833–1897)

Now known to many as one half of the rhyming slang for "drunk", in his early career Brahms earned a living playing **piano** in brothels around his native Hamburg. He continued to tour as a pianist and was regarded as a master of every type of music, except for **opera**, to which he never turned his hand.

- **Check out:** *Hungarian Dance No. 5 | Piano Concerto No. 1 | Symphony No. 4 | Violin Concerto*

Benjamin BRITTEN (1913-1976)

This composer has possibly the most appropriate sounding surname ever, as he seems to stand for everything that was Britain in the mid-20th century. For much of his life he lived in Aldeburgh, on the

Suffolk coast, where he founded the music festival that still continues every year in June.

- **Check out:** for a great introduction to Britten, try something like the *Sea Interludes* from *Peter Grimes* or the *Ceremony of Carols*

Max BRUCH (1838–1920)

This German composer is best known for his *Violin Concerto No. 1*. It's been voted the UK's favourite piece of classical music no fewer than five times in the annual Classic FM Hall of Fame poll. As well as composing, Bruch spent three years in Liverpool as the Music Director of the Royal Liverpool Philharmonic, now Classic FM's Orchestra in the North-West.

- **Check out:** *Scottish Fantasy* | *Kol Nidrei*

CELLO

This string instrument, played between the knees, comes between the **viola** and **double bass** in terms of pitch. It's more or less an oversized **violin**, although you shouldn't try getting one under your chin as the spike would certainly smart a bit. If you imagine the violin, viola, cello and double bass as being roughly the string equivalent of

soprano, **alto**, **tenor** and **bass**, respectively, then the cello is the heroic, hunky tenor.

- **Check out:** Jacqueline Du Pré | Julian Lloyd Webber | Steven Isserlis | Yo-Yo Ma

CHAMBER MUSIC

So called because it was written for groups small enough to play in the privacy of your own chamber, or room. Replaced nowadays by the Sony PlayStation. Chamber music can be for anything from a couple of soloists to larger chamber orchestras, which usually have up to 30 or so players. That's compared with a full symphony **orchestra**, which can have as many as 80 to 100 performers on the stage at any one time.

Frédéric CHOPIN (1810–1849)

Chopin was sort of the Henry Ford of composers, whose catchphrase might have been "you can have any instrument as long as it's the **piano**". Some would say he was a little obsessive about tinkling the ivories, writing no fewer than 169 different pieces for solo piano. And now for some trivia. His *Second Piano Concerto* was actually written before his *First Piano Concerto*. But his

First Piano Concerto was published first, so even though the *Second Piano Concerto* was in fact written first, it has always been referred to as the second.

- **Check out:** *Nocturne No. 2* | *Prelude No. 15 ('The Raindrop')* | *Waltz No. 6 ('The Minute Waltz'* – which, in fact, usually takes about a minute-and-a-half to play)

CHRISTMAS MUSIC

The tunes of some of the best-loved carols were, in fact, written by classical music greats (*Hark the herald* by **Mendelssohn**, *See amid the winter's snow* by **Holst**). As well as the hymns we sing each year, there's also a festive sack-load of longer pieces, such as the *Carol Symphony* by the exquisitely named Victor Hely-Hutchinson, which are perfect for having on in the background as the family arrive on Christmas Eve.

CLARINET

This is the most mellow of the woodwind instruments in the **orchestra**. When jazz and classical music meet, there's often a clarinet to be found somewhere towards the front of things.

CLASSICAL

Now, here's a funny one. Everything we play on Classic FM is classical music. But anything written between roughly 1750 and 1830 is described as coming from the "classical" period. This includes the work of **Haydn** and **Mozart**. **Beethoven**, too, wrote some music in the classical period but he also stayed on after the bell had gone for the early **romantic** period and wrote some stuff in that one too.

CONCERTO

A piece of music, usually in three **movements**, written for a solo instrument accompanied by an

orchestra. When a concerto is performed, the soloist, who is very much the star of the show, usually sits at the front of the stage next to the **conductor**.

CONDUCTOR

The human windmill waving the stick in front of an **orchestra**. A passable conductor can be the difference between a bad and a good performance. A great conductor can be the difference between a good and an unforgettable one. If you can't quite work out exactly what it is they do, imagine them in the same category as those new tights for women which support the bottom –

without them, things tend to go pear-shaped.

Aaron COPLAND (1900–1990)

This American composer's best-known work, *Fanfare for the Common Man*, provides a stirring brassy opening to many public events in the USA. At their inauguration, presidents swear by it.

- **Check out:** the ballet suites *Rodeo* and *Appalachian Spring*

COR ANGLAIS

This woodwind instrument is a slightly larger relative of the **oboe**. You can hear it playing the main tune in the slow movement of **Dvořák's** *New World Symphony* and playing the part of the swan in **Sibelius'** *The Swan of Tuonela.* Anybody who says they can tell it apart from an oboe is either (a) a genius, (b) a liar, or (c) a cor anglais player.

Claude DEBUSSY (1862–1918)

Debussy saw himself as a very French musician. He was friendly with many of the impressionist painters, which resulted in his work being given an "impressionist" tag. In fact, he wasn't really doing an impression of anyone – he was an innovator whose musical style paved the way for other 20th-century composers. His lover, Gaby, shot herself when he ended their relationship to set up home with his first wife, Rosalie. Gaby survived her suicide attempt. Five years later, he left Rosalie for his second wife. Just like Gaby, Rosalie shot herself and she, too, lived to tell the tale. The moral of this story? Never marry someone who's a good shot.

- **Check out:** *Clair de lune* | *La Mer* | *Prélude à l'après midi d'un Faune*

Léo DELIBES (1836–1891)

The Delibes **opera** *Lakmé* soared to new heights of popularity on the back of the long-running British Airways advertising campaign, which features the opera's most famous tune, the *Flower Duet.* His other popular composition is the ballet *Coppélia,* which tells the story of a toymaker and his dancing doll.

Frederick DELIUS (1862–1934)

Born in Bradford, Delius decided to become a composer in his twenties when he was running an orange plantation in Florida. In his latter years he suffered severely from the syphilis which he had picked up when in Paris in the 1890s. He was forced to dictate his music to his scribe, Eric Fenby, another Yorkshireman, without whom we'd have neither lots of the late Delius output, nor any knowledge of the word "amanuensis".

- **Check out:** *La Calinda* | *On Hearing the First Cuckoo in Spring* | *The Walk to the Paradise Garden*

DOUBLE BASS

Only the **harp** rivals this giant as the most difficult orchestral instrument to fit in the back of an estate car. Composers often use the deep sound of the double bass not just for its low, sonorous effect but also to add a little light relief to their music. For example, in **Saint-Saëns'** *Carnival of the Animals*, it plays the part of the elephant, another thing that it's difficult to get in the back of an estate car.

Antonín DVOŘÁK (1841–1904)

Dvořák loved his Czech homeland and was terribly homesick when he moved to the USA for three years in the 1890s. While he was there though, he discovered American folk melodies. These tunes heavily influenced him while he was writing his best-known work, the *New World Symphony* (*Symphony No. 9*). For many people in the UK though, the slow movement of this **symphony** will forever be associated with wholemeal bread and North Yorkshire streets, after it was used in adverts for Hovis.

- **Check out:** *Song to the Moon*

from the opera *Rusalka* | *Serenade for Strings* | *Slavonic Dances*

EARLY MUSIC

Any music that was composed before 1600 is said to be from the "early" period. Gregorian chant falls into this category (named after Pope Gregory who did much to develop church music), lots of which is very beautiful and relaxing.

Ludovico EINAUDI (born 1955)

This Italian pianist and composer is now a firm favourite with Classic FM listeners. He has become known particularly for his beautifully haunting melodies for solo **piano**.

- **Check out:** *Stanze* | *Le Onde* | *Eden Roc* | *I Giorni*

Sir Edward ELGAR (1857–1934)

One of the greatest British composers, Elgar is quite rightly regarded as a national treasure. He spent much of his life living in his native Worcestershire and the beautiful surrounding English countryside inspired him to write many of the most quintessentially English tunes. And his handlebar moustache is to die for. See for yourself by taking a look at the back of a twenty-pound note.

- **Check out:** *Cello Concerto* | *Chanson de matin* | *Pomp and*

Circumstance March No. 1 (the tune to 'Land of Hope and Glory') | *Salut d'amour* | *Serenade for Strings* | *Enigma Variations*, which includes the stirring *Nimrod*

Gabriel FAURÉ (1845–1924)

Best known for his *Requiem,* which is undoubtedly one of *the* great choral masterpieces, Fauré is far better known in his homeland, where he is more or less the French Elgar. His instrumental music is definitely worth a listen.

- **Check out:** *Pavane* | *Cantique de Jean Racine* | *Dolly Suite*

FILM MUSIC

There's a long history of music being used in films, right back to the days when a pianist would accompany silent movies with a live performance. Many of the greatest pieces of classical music by composers as varied as **Mozart**, **Beethoven** and **Wagner** have been used in films. Add to this a long tradition of composers being commissioned to write music especially for the cinema and we're talking quite a large section in the record shop. **Saint-Saëns**, **Copland**, **Vaughan Williams**, **Walton**, **Prokofieff** and **Shostakovich** all have soundtracks to their names.

More recently, Howard **Shore**, John **Barry**, James Horner and Hans **Zimmer** have all given the undoubted king of movie composers, John **Williams**, a run for his money.

FLUTE

This is at the smaller end of the woodwind family. It's still classed as woodwind even though it's usually made from metal. The Irishman James Galway shot to fame as "the man with the golden flute" in the 1970s and 1980s and he remains one of the best-known flautists today. Among the flute's good points – it's perfect for kids to take up, being small enough to be carried to school. Among the bad points, it's very easy to leave on the bus.

César FRANCK (1822–1890)

Here is one of those rarest of beasts – a famous Belgian. And unlike Hercule Poirot or Tintin, César Franck actually existed. He never really had much success with his music during his life. In fact, the first glimmer of critical approval only came in the weeks before he died.

- **Check out**: *Panis Angelicus* | *Symphonic Variations for Piano and Orchestra*

FRENCH HORN

A member of the brass family, if this instrument was uncoiled it would not only stretch for more than three metres, it would also give you something to do on a Sunday afternoon. Best not attempted during the quiet bit in a concert, though. Great composers for the horn include **Mozart** and Richard **Strauss**.

George GERSHWIN
(1898–1937)

Despite being written in the early part of the 20th century, Gershwin's music sounds very fresh and contemporary today. He was the master of fusing together jazz and classical music and was earning as much as $250,000 a year at the height of his popularity, which must make him one of the most financially successful of any composer in their own lifetime.

- **Check out:** *Rhapsody in Blue* | *Piano Concerto in F* | his opera *Porgy and Bess* which includes the hit songs 'Summertime' and 'I got Plenty o' Nuttin'

Philip GLASS (born 1937)

Arguably one of the most respected living American composers, Glass' music receives its widest audience through his **film** soundtracks.

- **Check out:** *Violin Concerto* | *Koyaanisqatsi* | *The Hours* | *Kundun*

Henryk GÓRECKI (born 1933)

This Polish composer shot to fame back in 1992 when Classic FM started to play a recording of his *Symphony No. 3* featuring the soprano Dawn Upshaw with the London Sinfonietta. The second **movement** of this '*Symphony of Sorrowful Songs*' is a particular favourite. None of his other music has come anywhere close to repeating this success. And don't let the name catch you out – even though it doesn't look like it, it's pronounced "Goretski".

Charles GOUNOD (1818–1893)

Gounod was writing music in Paris at the time when it was a seething hotbed of great **romantic** composers. His contemporaries include **Chopin**, **Liszt** and **Berlioz**. His most famous work is the **opera** *Faust*, which spawned the *Jewel Song* and *The Soldiers' Chorus*. But Classic FM listeners' favourite Gounod piece has proved to be *Judex* from his little-known **oratorio** *Mors et Vita*.

- **Check out:** *Ave Maria* (Gounod borrowed Bach's *Prelude No. 1* and put a second tune over the top of it)

Edvard GRIEG (1843–1907)

Grieg is Norway's most famous musical son, although the Scots could lay some claim to him being one of their own because his Scottish great-grandfather emigrated to Scandinavia after the Battle of Culloden. Many of his tunes contain soaring melodies that evoke his Norwegian home.

- **Check out:** *Piano Concerto* | *Holberg Suite* | *Peer Gynt Suites Nos. 1 and 2* (the first includes the hits *Morning* and *In the Hall of the Mountain King*)

GUITAR

The guitar in classical music is not quite the macho, trendy "axe" of its rock music cousin. In fact, next to a full **orchestra**, it has to fight to be heard, and is more often found in smaller groups or played solo. That's not to say there aren't some great guitar and orchestra pieces, **Rodrigo's** *Concierto de Aranjuez* being one of the most popular.

George Frideric HANDEL (1685–1759)

Handel was the Greg Rusedski of classical music. Although he was German, he was considered one of

Britain's great composers, after becoming a British citizen. This came to pass when his boss the Elector of Hanover was promoted to the job of being King George I. His music includes **opera** and instrumental work, but he's probably best known for his great big choral masterpieces, which are still regularly performed up and down the country today.

- **Check out:** *Messiah* | 'Ombra mai fu' from the opera *Xerxes* | *Zadok the Priest* (used in the film *The Madness of King George*) | *Water Music* | *Music for the Royal Fireworks* | *Arrival of the Queen of Sheba* from the oratorio *Solomon*

HARP

It may make a heavenly noise but carrying it is a hell of a job. One of the hardest orchestral instruments to play, the harp nevertheless makes a beautiful sound.

- **Not to be confused with:** Harmonica (mouth organ) players often refer to their instruments as the "harp". Don't muddle the two types of harp – it could hurt

Joseph HAYDN (1732–1809)

Now to say that Haydn was hard-working would be a dramatic understatement. During the 77 years of his life he wrote no fewer than 104

symphonies, more than 80 string quartets, over 50 piano **sonatas**, at least 24 **concertos** and 20 **operas**. And we haven't even got started on the choral and **chamber** pieces yet.

- **Check out:** the magnificent choral work *The Creation* | *Symphony No. 94 in G,* known as the '*Surprise Symphony*' because of the deafening chord that comes crashing in after a very quiet opening | *Cello Concertos Nos. 1 & 2* | *The Seasons*

Gustav HOLST (1874–1934)

One of those One-Hit-Wonders, Gustav Holst is famous for writing *The Planets.* Six of the seven **movements** represent the astrological influences of the planets: *Mars* (war), *Venus* (peace), *Jupiter* (jollity), *Uranus* (magic), *Saturn* (old age) and *Neptune* (mysticism). The other movement is reserved for *Mercury*, the winged messenger of the gods. Pluto fails to make the line up, mainly because it had not yet been discovered. The great hymn and rugby anthem 'I vow to thee my country' is sung to the tune of *Jupiter.*

INCIDENTAL MUSIC

Stretching back to ancient Greek times, incidental music is the fore-runner to the **film** soundtrack. As in **Grieg's** music to Ibsen's play *Peer*

Gynt, it was often written to add atmosphere to the action on a stage or even to fill in the sections where the director thought "What shall we do in this bit where nothing's going on?" If nothing else, incidental music lets the audience know that now is really not the time to nip out for a choc-ice.

INTERMEZZO

This is the operatic equivalent of your TV screen going all soft focus and a caption reading "Ten Years Later" appearing. Don't you just hate it when that happens? Well, an intermezzo is a piece of orchestral music in the middle of an **opera**, which is used to show the audience that a period of time has gone by. But, oddly enough, it's no where near as annoying as a "Ten Years Later" caption.

Karl JENKINS (born 1944)

Karl Jenkins has had a varied career, ranging from being principal oboist in the National Youth Orchestra to being a leading member of the seventies' rock outfit Soft Machine. *Adiemus: Songs of Sanctuary* was an instant hit with Classic FM listeners back in 1995 and, like much of Jenkins' music, has become even more famous by being used in TV advertising campaigns.

- **Check out:** *The Armed Man: A Mass for Peace* | *Palladio*

Aram KHACHATURIAN (1903–1978)

Two pieces of music written for separate ballets top the list of this Armenian composer's most played work. The *Sabre Dance* from *Gayaneh* may have made him famous around the globe just after it was written in the 1940s, but for a whole generation he will always be the man behind the theme tune to *The Onedin Line.* This piece's real name is the *Adagio of Spartacus and Phrygia.*

LEGATO

Another one of those Italian instructions from composers to musicians – this time they are asking the performer to play smoothly. The opposite is *staccato* – a rather spikier sound.

Franz LISZT (1811–1886)

One of the great pianists of his time, a performance by Liszt was greeted by the sort of response that we would associate with a chart-topping pop superstar today. He enjoyed the rock 'n' roll lifestyle a good century before it had been invented and had a long list of sexual conquests – even after he took holy orders.

- **Check out:** *Hungarian Rhapsody No. 2* | *Liebestraum No. 3* | *Piano Sonata* | *Rhapsodie Espagnole*

Gustav MAHLER (1860–1911)

A renowned **conductor** during his lifetime, particularly of **opera**, Mahler only rose to real popularity as a composer during the latter half of the 20th century. He was a tortured soul who was analysed by Freud. His biggest hit is the *Adagietto* from his *Symphony No. 5.* He wrote nine **symphonies**, which seems to be THE number to write – **Beethoven** and **Dvořák** also wrote nine.

- **Check out:** *Symphony No. 1* (known as '*The Titan*') | *Symphony*

No. 2 (*'The Resurrection'*) | *Symphony No. 8* (known as *'The Symphony of a Thousand'* because of the vast number of musicians needed to perform it)

Pietro MASCAGNI (1863–1945)

This Italian One-Hit-Wonder is best known for his **opera** *Cavalleria Rusticana.* But rather than a famous **aria**, it's the ***Intermezzo*** (the bit in the middle) that is most often heard today. When this opera is performed in full, it tends to be paired up with another One-Hit-Wonder, Leoncavallo's *I Pagliacci* – a double act known as *Cav & Pag*.

Jules MASSENET (1842–1912)

Much like **Mascagni**, Massenet is most famous for a piece of **incidental** music from an **opera** – this time, it's the gentle *Meditation* from *Thaïs*. Sadly, as far as we know, he never wrote a "mass in A", thus depriving the world of Massenet's Mass in A. Which, were it to receive an afternoon performance, would be Massenet's Mass in A matinee.

Sir Paul McCARTNEY (born 1942)

The former Beatle is one of the greatest-ever pop music composers and when, a few years ago, he turned his hand to classical music he proved that his knack for writing a strong, catchy melody had not deserted him.

- **Check out:** *Liverpool Oratorio* | *The Leaf* | *Standing Stone* | *Working Classical*

Felix MENDELSSOHN (1809–1847)

This German-born composer was a frighteningly clever child, excelling as a painter, poet, athlete, linguist, and musician. He made his public debut as a pianist at the age of nine and by the time he was sixteen he had composed his *Octet for Strings*. A tour of Scotland in 1829 resulted in his hugely popular *Hebrides Overture.* His music tends to be bright and cheerful but he died at a tragically young age, only 38, having never really recovered from the death of his much-loved sister, Fanny, who was also a gifted musician.

- **Check out:** the *Wedding March* from *A Midsummer Night's Dream*, which remains a popular choice at the end of marriage services | *O for the wings of a dove* | *Songs without Words* | *Symphony No. 4* ('*Italian*') | *Violin Concerto*

Modest MOUSSORGSKY (1839–1881)

Moussorgsky was a high-ranking official in the Russian guards and his story is one of riches to rags. As a young adult, he was quite a man about town, but, by the time he died at the age of 42, he had descended into alcohol-induced poverty. Hence in the most common picture of him, he has a bright red nose.

- **Check out:** *Pictures at an Exhibition* | *Night on the Bare Mountain*, used in Walt Disney's *Fantasia*

MOVEMENT

In music, a movement does not refer to the stampede towards the bar at the interval of a concert. Instead, it is one section of a bigger piece.

Usually different movements are played at different speeds, indicated by those Italian instructions of which composers are so fond.

Wolfgang Amadeus MOZART
(1756–1791)

When those in the know sit down to debate "Who's the greatest of them all?" Mozart and **Beethoven** usually end up coming first and second, although the top spot changes hands as often as a magician's playing card. Probably the best-known child prodigy, Mozart could play the keyboard by the age of 3 and could compose from 5. He went on his first European tour when he was 6 and by the time he had reached the grand old age of 12, he had finished two **operas**. His music is an excellent choice if you're planning to go to a live classical concert for the first time. It's nice to know that he did have some faults though – he was said to be very arrogant, had a strange obsession with his rear end and was hopeless at managing his money. Oh, and his head was too big.

- **Check out:** *Laudate Dominum* | *Requiem* | *Clarinet Concerto in A* | *Piano Concerto No. 21* | *Horn Concerto No. 4* | *Piano Concerto No. 24* | *Serenade No. 13* (*'Eine kleine Nachtmusik'*) | *Symphony*

No. 41 ('Jupiter') | *Così fan tutte* | *Don Giovanni* | *The Magic Flute* | *The Marriage of Figaro* | the film *Amadeus*

NOCTURNE

Written for the **piano**, these short pieces were invented by the Irish composer John Field. **Chopin** then developed the idea further. They are perfect to listen to as a late evening wind-down, as they are intended to suggest the calm of the night.

Michael NYMAN (born 1944)

This British composer has written many **film** soundtracks, the best known of which is *The Piano*. He later turned the score into a single movement *Piano Concerto.*

OBOE

A black, wooden wind instrument, that looks a bit like a **clarinet** with a straw sticking out of the top. It has a more "nasal" sound than the clarinet, but, played well, can sound utterly beautiful. Played badly, it can bring to mind Sweep from "The Sooty Show" being attacked by geese. Either way, its piercing sound can always be heard through everything else. It's also the instrument you hear before an orchestral concert, playing the note to which all the other instruments tune.

Jacques OFFENBACH
(1819–1880)

This is the man who let loose the Can-Can on an unsuspecting public back in 1858. It comes from *Orpheus in the Underworld*, which scandalised the chattering classes of Paris at the time of its premiere. Offenbach is also known for the *Barcarolle* from his **opera** *The Tales of Hoffman*. There used to be a strange association of bad luck attached to his name, a bit like Macbeth in the theatre, whereby people would have to cross themselves if he was mentioned.

OPERA

Operas tend to be big on great tunes, passion, sorrow, romance and drama. Sadly, they are rarely big on plot. Opera storylines tend to centre around either unrequited love, or bizarre "what do you mean you're really a horse in disguise" madness. Broadly speaking though, most opera storylines go something like this: *Man falls in love with woman. Woman turns out to be either related or someone she claimed not to be. Man and woman's love doomed. Cue angst (in song). Woman (can be man – doesn't matter) dies horrific death, preferably involving consumption. Remaining lover dies.*

Big song. End. Everyone goes down the pub. In fact, opera is really what classical music would be like if Quentin Tarantino had invented it. But despite the high body count, it has given us some of the most spectacular and beautiful pieces anywhere in classical music.

OPUS

The Italian word for "work". In other words, this is simply a database of a composer's work in chronological order. So *Opus 3* would be the third piece that a composer had written. **Mozart** and **J.S. Bach** have their own numbering systems. Mozart's was done by Ludwig von Köchel, who, being a shy and retiring sort of chap, decided to give each of Mozart's works a Köchel number instead of an Opus number. In J.S. Bach's case, his pieces all have *BWV* in front of the number. These initials stand for *Bach Werke-Verzeichnis*, which is German for "Catalogue of Bach's Works", and are not, as some think, a "best before" date mark.

ORATORIO

Often staged in a church or cathedral, an oratorio is a religious story set to music and performed by solo singers, a choir and an **orchestra**. Usually though, the story is told without scenery and costumes – so the event is more of a concert. In the end, it's a bit like **opera**, only cheaper.

ORCHESTRA

Imagine. Four different types of instruments – some thirty string players alone, as well as ten or so brass, around the same number of woodwind, and a liberal sprinkling of percussionists. Seventy-odd different players in all, spread out over a space the size of a tennis court, all being told what to do by a guy (or girl) who might never have played a note in his (or her) life. Shouldn't work, should it? But it does. Amazing.

Carl ORFF (1895–1982)

Carl Orff's *Carmina Burana* sniffed out the sweet smell of popularity after advertising executives decided that the opening 'O fortuna' would be the perfect accompaniment to the crashing waves of an advertising campaign for Old Spice aftershave. And although it might sound all medieval and gothic, Orff died so recently that he may in fact have seen the Old Spice ad on the telly. Who knows? He himself may have splashed some on.

ORGAN

Known as "The King of Instruments", these mighty beasts demand that

orchestras and audiences come to them. Many organ performances take place in cathedrals or churches, although there are some concert halls with permanent built-in organs. The organ is played not only with the hands, but also the feet, which get their own "shoe-sized" keyboard under the main organ.

OVERTURE

The bit that comes at the beginning of an **opera**. It's very often a sort of greatest hits showcase of the tunes that will follow, although sometimes composers write an overture that doesn't have anything else coming afterwards. The most famous example of this is Tchaikovsky's *1812 Overture*.

Johann PACHELBEL (1653–1706)

Another One-Hit-Wonder, this organist and composer is famous for his *Canon*. Just like **Albinoni's** *Adagio*, it only became mega-well-known more than a couple of hundred years after it was written. But, unlike Albinoni, it was at least all his own work.

Arvo PÄRT (born 1935)

This Estonian composer sits alongside John **Tavener**, Henryk

Górecki and John **Rutter** as one of the most popular modern choral writers. His laid-back, gentle sound is the musical equivalent of an empty, white room and appeals to "chillout" enthusiasts just as much as to classical fans. To pronounce his name correctly, imagine a "pear" then add a soft "t".

- **Check out:** *Spiegel im Spiegel*

PERCUSSION

Orchestral instruments that you either hit or shake. They include the timpani (or kettledrums), cymbals, glockenspiel, xylophone, marimba, triangle, tambourine, castanets, tubular bells, side drum and bass drum. The percussion section also provides some of the more unusual sound effects that a composer can ask for, such as car horns, wind machines and car suspension springs. Britain's best-known percussionist is Evelyn Glennie.

PIANO

Invented in Florence, around 1709, modern-day pianos come in many shapes and sizes. "Piano" is short for "pianoforte", which is the Italian for "quiet loud". It's one of the few instruments that can play lots of notes at once – so virtually every composer wrote some great stuff for the piano.

Zbigniew PREISNER
(born 1955)

When the *Requiem for my Friend* was released in 1996, it became an instant hit with Classic FM listeners. The friend in the title is the Polish **film** director Krzystof Kieslowski, he of the *Three Colours* trilogy fame, for whose movies Preisner had written the music.

Serge PROKOFIEFF
(1891–1953)

This Russian composer suffered at the hands of Stalin, facing charges of composing music that worked against the State. Despite this, not only did he stay on in his homeland, he also left us with many great tunes. Some were influenced by the time he spent in America and Europe during the early part of his adult life.

- **Check out:** *Sleigh Ride (Troika)* from the *Lieutenant Kijé Suite* | *The Montagues and Capulets* from the ballet *Romeo and Juliet,* which accompanies Sunderland footballers on to the pitch each week | *Peter and the Wolf*

Giacomo PUCCINI (1858–1924)

Puccini took the **opera** baton from **Verdi** and ran with it, writing hit **aria** after hit aria. *La Bohème*, *Tosca* and *Madam Butterfly* are quite possibly the three most performed operas today. He also penned the aria that, for many people, simply *is* opera – 'Nessun Dorma' from *Turandot*. This song, made famous by The Three Tenors at the 1990 World Cup Finals in Italy, brought classical music into millions of people's lives.

- **Check out:** 'Che gelida manina' and 'O soave fanciulla' from *La Bohème* | 'O mio babbino caro' from *Gianni Schicchi* | 'Un bel di' and *The Humming Chorus* from *Madam Butterfly* | 'Vissi d'arte' from *Tosca*

Henry PURCELL (1659–1695)

Often referred to as the first great English composer, Purcell was an amazing young talent, becoming Organist of Westminster Abbey – a top job – by the time he was 20. Despite the fact that he only lived for another 16 years, he had a busy old time of it, composing every conceivable type of music.

- **Check out:** 'When I am laid in earth' (known as '*Dido's Lament*') from *Dido and Aeneas* | the *Rondo* from *Abdelazar* | *Trumpet Tune and Air in D*

Serge RACHMANINOFF
(1873–1943)

Rachmaninoff was one of those annoying people who wasn't just brilliant at one thing – he was top of the pile in three different areas. Today, we remember him as a composer, but in his day he was a fine **conductor** and a magnificent concert pianist. His *Piano Concerto No. 2* has consistently been voted number one in the Classic FM Hall of Fame and his *Piano Concerto No. 3* shot to stardom after being included in the **film** *Shine*. He's also known for having one of the largest pairs of hands in classical music, which is why some of his **piano** pieces are fiendishly difficult for less well-endowed performers. Despite his success, Rachmaninoff seldom smiled in the photographs he left behind. Perhaps the Russians have no word for "cheese".

- **Check out:** *Rhapsody on a Theme of Paganini* | *Symphony No. 2* | *Vocalise*

Maurice RAVEL (1875–1937)

A whole generation of people came across Ravel's music for the first time when Torvill and Dean skated their way to a gold medal accompanied by the *Bolero*. During World War 1, Ravel enlisted as an ambulance driver. He was deeply affected by the death and destruction that he witnessed, and the poignant *Le tombeau de Couperin* was his tribute not only to the French composer Couperin, but also to his fallen comrades.

- **Check out:** *Pavane pour une infante défunte* | the ballet *Daphnis and Chloé* | *Piano Concerto in G* | *Piano Concerto for left hand* which was written for a friend who lost an arm in World War 1

Nikolai RIMSKY-KORSAKOFF (1844–1908)

A Russian naval officer turned music professor, Rimsky-Korsakoff is best known for *Scheherezade,* which is based on the story of *The Arabian Nights*. When it came to knowing how to write brilliantly for **orchestra**, Rimsky-Korsakoff was in a league of his own and also made quite a name for himself by arranging the work of other composers.

- **Check out:** *Flight of the Bumble Bee* | *Capriccio Espagnol*

Joaquín RODRIGO (1901–1999)

The *Concierto de Aranjuez* is this Spanish composer's greatest hit outside of his home country. It's also the most popular piece for **guitar** and **orchestra**, having been "covered" by so many different people, from Miles Davis to the Grimethorpe Colliery Brass Band (as *Concerto de Orange Juice* in the **film** *Brassed Off!*).

ROMANTIC

Love features heavily in classical music, just as it does in pop. But, in this case, "romantic" refers to the composers who were writing music from roughly 1830 to 1900, including **Schubert**, **Chopin** and **Berlioz**.

Gioachino ROSSINI
(1792–1868)

Another of the great Italian **opera** composers, Rossini was a one-man-hit factory until he was 37. Then, suddenly, he stopped writing opera altogether and for the last thirty years of his life his only really major work was the choral piece *Stabat Mater*. Nobody is quite sure why. Still, by then he had racked up enormous success at home and abroad. Food was also important to him, and his recipe for "Tournedos Rossini" is still popular today.

- **Check out:** 'Largo al factotum' from *The Barber of Seville* | Overture to *The Silken Ladder* | Overture to *The Thieving Magpie* | Overture to *William Tell*

John RUTTER (born 1945)

John Rutter's music is probably performed more often and in more places around Britain than any other living British classical composer. Based in Cambridge, his choral anthems and carols have become a major part of church services in this country. His most famous work is his stunningly beautiful *Requiem*, which is often performed by amateur choral groups.

- **Check out :** *A Gaelic Blessing*, often referred to by mischievous choirboys as '*A Garlic Dressing*' | *For the Beauty of the Earth*

Camille SAINT-SAËNS
(1835–1921)

To say that Saint-Saëns was a clever kid is an understatement. This book is full of child stars, but he was probably the most prodigious of the lot. He could read and write and play tunes on the **piano** at the age of just two. By the age of seven he was something of an expert in lepidoptery, (the study of insects to us mere mortals). His best-known piece is *The Carnival of the Animals*, which he banned from being performed during his lifetime in case people stopped taking him seriously. The animal theme continues, albeit unwittingly, with his other famous work, his *'Organ' Symphony No. 3*, which will forever be linked to "sheep-pigs", after being used in the **film** *Babe*.

Erik SATIE (1866–1925)

This French composer is best known for his *Gymnopédies Nos. 1* and *3* for **piano**. He was something of an eccentric and had a habit of giving many of his pieces ridiculous names.

Waltz of the Chocolate with Almonds and *Three Pear-Shaped Pieces* are not often heard today.

SAXOPHONE

The coolest of the wind instruments, **Debussy**, **Vaughan-Williams**, **Berlioz**, **Bizet** and Glazunov have all written pieces featuring the sax. Their popularity has been somewhat overshadowed recently by 'Parce Mihi Domine' from the album *Officium*, a collaboration between the jazz saxophonist Jan Garbarek and the early music vocal group, the Hilliard Ensemble. The sound that they create is crossover music at its very best.

Franz SCHUBERT (1797–1828)

Some composers seem to find one thing and stick to it like glue. If Schubert is salt, then songs (or, as he would have said, *Lieder*) are pepper. Despite dying at the age of 31, he composed more than 600 of them. To be fair, he also found time for more or less nine **symphonies** (one was unfinished), eleven **operas** and hundreds of other pieces. In his day, he was famous for his musical parties known as *Schubertiads*.

- **Check out:** *Marche Militaire No. 1* | Overture and Incidental Music to *Rosamunde* | *Piano Quintet* ('*Trout*') based on one of his songs | *Piano*

Sonata No. 21 | *Symphony No. 8 ('Unfinished')*

Robert SCHUMANN (1810–1856)

Schumann was a great composer, but as a performer he lived in the shadow of his wife Clara, a renowned concert pianist. He suffered from syphilis and depression, and attempted suicide by throwing himself into the Rhine at the age of 44. Two years later, he died in an asylum.

- **Check out:** *Scenes from Childhood No. 7 – Dreaming* | *Fantasie in C* | *Piano Concerto in A minor* | the song-cycle *Dichterliebe*

Howard SHORE (born 1946)

This Canadian **film** composer has soared in popularity following the release of his soundtrack to the film version of *The Lord of the Rings* in 2001. He has also written the music to the two sequels.

Dmitri SHOSTAKOVICH (1906–1975)

Among the greatest of 20th-century composers, Shostakovich spent his entire life falling in and out of favour with the ruling Communist Party in Russia. Despite the pressure over what sort of music he should compose, he still managed to write a stack of hits. He was also one of the first great **film** composers – with many of his movie scores still being performed today.

- **Check out:** *Jazz Suites Nos. 1 and 2* | *Romance* from *The Gadfly* | *The Assault on Beautiful Gorky* | *Symphony No. 5* | *Piano Concerto No. 2*

Jean SIBELIUS (1865–1957)

He may have looked like a rather grumpy Kojak, with his shaven head and lollipop, but in his native Finland he was a musical hero. Many of his best-loved works are heavily influenced by the folk music of his homeland. He liked to drink and to smoke and was diagnosed as suffering from throat cancer in his forties. The operations to remove the malignant growths were successful and he lived for another half a century. More than twenty years before he died, having made enough money to live comfortably, he simply stopped composing and retired. Oh, and we lied about the lollipop.

- **Check out:** *Karelia Suite* | *The Swan of Tuonela* | *Finlandia* | *Valse Triste* | *Violin Concerto* | *Symphony No. 2*

Bedřich SMETANA (1824–1884)

Smetana ended up suffering from deafness, syphilis and ultimately going completely mad. Before then, he made his name as the father of Czech musical nationalism. His most popular piece, *Vltava* from *Ma Vlast* (*My Homeland*) is about the passage of the River Vltava to the sea. His other big hit is the overture to his **opera** *The Bartered Bride*.

SONATA

A piece of music usually written either for a solo instrument, or for any single instrument with a **piano**. It's written in three or four **movements** and follows a set of rules so complicated, it would make the Civil Service jealous.

SOPRANO

Sopranos are the highest female voices providing not only the female lead but also, more often than not, the love-interest for the male **tenors** in **opera**. Sopranos often heard on Classic FM include Maria Callas, Renée Fleming, Lesley Garrett and Angela Gheorghiu. Mezzo-sopranos, such as Cecilia Bartoli, have voices that are slightly deeper.

STRAUSS FAMILY

This is one of the great dynasties of classical music, something along the lines of what Kirk and Michael Douglas are to acting today. Johann

Strauss Senior was born in 1804 and his son, Johann Strauss Junior, came into the world 19 years later. Dad's best-known work is the infectiously-fun *Radetzky March*, while the younger man gave us a whole host of waltzes, including the most popular of them all, *The Blue Danube*. There was another son, Josef, who composed more than 280 pieces, but who has been eclipsed by the other two.

Richard STRAUSS (1864–1949)

No relation to the Viennese Strauss family, Richard Strauss is best known for *Also sprach Zarathustra*, which was used in the Stanley

Kubrick **film** *2001: A Space Odyssey*. He is regarded as one of the last great German **romantics** despite the fact that he was writing on well into the 20th century. His international standing fell when he decided to continue working in Germany after 1939, although at the end of World War 2 he was acquitted of being a Nazi collaborator.

- **Check out:** *Der Rosenkavalier* | *Four Last Songs*

Igor STRAVINSKY (1882–1971)

One of the great composers of the 20th century, this Russian caused a storm during his lifetime because of the innovative style of his music.

He's something of a rent-a-quote, having said some "bon mot" about virtually every aspect of music at some point – a sort of Groucho Marx of classical music.

- **Check out:** *The Rite of Spring*, which literally caused a riot at its premiere | *The Firebird*, which has one of the best finales anywhere in classical music

SYMPHONY

This is a large-scale piece, normally written for an **orchestra**. It usually has four separate **movements**, and was once considered the greatest challenge to which a composer could aspire. Like buses, they rarely come in ones. Having said that, unlike buses, they seem to come in nines – **Beethoven**, **Schubert** and **Mahler** each wrote nine of them.

John TAVENER (born 1944)

John Tavener's music reached its biggest-ever audience when his *Song for Athene* was used at the end of the funeral service held at Westminster Abbey for Diana, Princess of Wales. In the 1980s he wrote *The Protecting Veil* for the cellist Steven Isserlis and more recently found his choral piece *The Lamb* being used on TV to sell mobile phones.

- **Not to be confused with:** John Taverner, with two "r"s, an English composer of sacred music born some 450 years earlier than John Tavener, one "r"

Peter TCHAIKOVSKY
(1840–1893)

One of the greatest of all composers, Tchaikovsky led a tortured life. He suffered from depression and was suicidal on more than one occasion. He was driven to despair by the poor reception given to his early compositions (many of which are now huge hits) and by guilt over his homosexuality, which was socially unacceptable at the time. His benefactor throughout his life was a rich widow, who insisted they never actually meet. There is confusion over exactly how he died – officially, cholera from infected water claimed his life, although there is some evidence that he may have drunk it knowingly. Tchaikovsky had a knack for great tunes and lots of them. His ballets are among the most often performed today.

- **Check out:** *The Nutcracker* | *1812 Overture* | *Piano Concerto No. 1* | *Symphony No. 6 ('Pathétique')* | *Romeo and Juliet* | *The Sleeping Beauty* | *Swan Lake*

TENOR

Tenors are generally the "heroes" of the **opera** world, getting many of the best male **arias**. Their voices are higher than **baritones** and **basses**. The most well-known are *The Three Tenors* – Luciano Pavarotti, José Carreras and Placido Domingo – a trio who have become multi-millionaires on the back of their stadium concerts around the globe.

TROMBONE

The sliding metal tube on a trombone not only lengthens or shortens the pipework to give the instrument a different pitch, it also gives it its "comedy" value, providing that somewhat *Carry On . . .* sound. They are the powerhouses of the brass section of the **orchestra**.

TRUMPET

This is the best-known member of the brass family, with a long history stretching back to biblical times. It is more agile than the **trombone** because it has three buttons (valves) instead of a slide. Its ability to be heard over a church **organ** has made it very popular at weddings.

Jay UNGAR (born 1946)

This American composer became a star when a superb arrangement of his tune *The Ashokan Farewell* was played on Classic FM. There was a huge response from listeners to the piece, which was used as the theme to a television documentary called *The American Civil War.* It has now rocketed into the Top 10 of the annual Classic FM Hall of Fame listener vote. So far, Ungar resolutely remains a One-Hit-Wonder.

Ralph VAUGHAN WILLIAMS
(1872–1958)

The music of Ralph Vaughan Williams is as English as warm beer and cricket on the village green. Born in Gloucestershire, he collected traditional English folk songs from a young age and it's these tunes which went on to provide him with the core of many of his subsequent hits. Since Classic FM began broadcasting in 1992, the popularity of Vaughan Williams has grown steadily each year. By the way, "Ralph", in this instance, is pronounced to rhyme with "safe", as in the actor Ralph Fiennes.

- **Check out:** *Fantasia on a Theme of Thomas Tallis* | *The Lark Ascending* | *English Folk Song Suite* | *Fantasia on Greensleeves* | *Symphony No. 2 ('London')*

Giuseppe VERDI (1813–1901)

The fact that when we think of Italy, we think of **opera**, is in no small part down to this mischievous-looking man, considered by many to be the greatest of all Italian opera composers. Big tuneful hits fill his 26 operas and the majority of them remain on the bill of fare at opera houses around the world today. His other major work, the *Requiem*, is regarded as one of the greatest pieces of choral music ever written.

- **Check out:** 'Celeste Aida' and *The Grand March* from *Aida* | Overture to *La Forza Del Destino* | 'Questa o quella' and 'La donna e mobile' from *Rigoletto* | 'Sempre libera' from *La Traviata* | *Anvil Chorus* from *Il Trovatore* | *Chorus of the Hebrew Slaves* from *Nabucco* | 'Dies Irae' from the *Requiem*

VIOLA

Often the butt of jokes among professional musicians, the viola looks just like a **violin**, but is slightly bigger, makes a deeper sound and burns for longer when you set fire to it. That's the punchline to one of the jokes, by the way.

VIOLIN

There is safety in numbers if you are a violin player in an **orchestra**: around twenty to thirty other people sitting next to you playing the same instrument, all following the leader (the one at the front, nearest the **conductor**). Virtuoso violinists most often played on Classic FM include Nigel Kennedy, Anne-Sophie Mutter, Maxim Vengerov and Chloë Hanslip.

Antonio VIVALDI (1678–1741)

Despite the fact that Vivaldi wrote somewhere around 800 different works, his music was rarely played from his death in 1741 right through to the middle of the 20th century. He then had something of a comeback and now sits near the top of the list of most-performed **baroque** composers. Were there to be a "Musical Redheads Hall of Fame", he'd be up there with Cilla Black and Mick Hucknall. Even though he was a priest, he used to tour with both a top **soprano** *and* her sister. Despite his denials, everyone thought that there was more to this threesome than just trio sonatas. And they say blondes have all the fun.

- **Check out:** *Four Seasons* | *Gloria* | *Nulla in Mundo Pax Sincera*, used in the film *Shine*

Richard WAGNER (1813–1883)

Think Wagner, think "extreme". His music was extreme, and it tends to elicit extreme reactions from listeners. It's love or hate with him. People rarely use the word "quite" in connection with Wagner. Despite his genius, he was a deeply flawed character – racist, anti-Semitic, a

Machiavellian serial philanderer with a monstrous ego. Sound awful? Well, try the music before you make up your mind. His greatest achievement is the four **operas** that make up *The Ring* cycle, which together last for more than 20 hours. No, that's not a misprint.

- **Check out:** Overture to *The Flying Dutchman* | Prelude to Act 1 of *Lohengrin* | *Bridal Chorus* from *Lohengrin* | *Ride of the Valkyries* from *Die Walküre*, which was used as American helicopters swooped into Vietnam in *Apocalypse Now* | *Siegfried's Funeral March* from *Götterdämmerung* | *Pilgrims' Chorus* from *Tannhäuser* | Prelude to *Tristan and Isolde*

William WALTON (1902–1983)

If **Vaughan Williams'** music can evoke a picture of pastoral England, then Walton is able to convey the majesty – the "pomp" to Vaughan-Williams' "circumstance". Pieces such as *Crown Imperial* and *Orb and Sceptre* seem to be written in the key of ermine.

- **Check out:** *Spitfire Prelude and Fugue* | his *Henry V Suite*, written for Laurence Olivier's 1944 film

Charles-Marie WIDOR (1844–1937)

During his time, Widor (pronounced Vee Door) was the David Beckham of the **organ** world – a truly dazzling player. His *Organ Symphony No. 5*, and in particular the *Toccata* which ends it, has become a big part of many wedding ceremonies.

John WILLIAMS (born 1932)

Arguably the greatest living **film** composer. If a movie has a John Williams soundtrack, it nearly always means that it's a Hollywood blockbuster. His hit list includes *Star Wars*, *Harry Potter*, *Schindler's List*, *Superman* and *E.T.*

- **Not to be confused with:** the other John Williams, a brilliant classical guitarist

Hans ZIMMER (born 1957)

Another movie composer, Hans Zimmer is known principally for his soundtrack to *Gladiator*, although he had early success as the writer of TV theme tunes.

Domenico ZIPOLI (1688–1726)

Until the premiere of **Zimmer's** *Gladiator*, this organist and composer's main job was to be the chief "Z" in classical music. He hailed from Naples, but towards the end of his life he got the travel bug and emigrated to Argentina. His one surviving hit is *Elevazione*, which has become a big favourite for Classic FM listeners.